MW00916711

The Tao of Male Sex Appeal

by

Jim Carrera and Sean Marsh

authorHOUSE

1663 LIBERTY DRIVE, SUITE 200
BLOOMINGTON, INDIANA 47403
(800) 839-8640
www.authorhouse.com

First published by AuthorHouse 07/14/04

ISBN: 1-4184-0414-4 (e)
ISBN: 1-4184-0415-2 (sc)

Printed in the United States of America
Bloomington, Indiana

This book is printed on acid-free paper.

Table of Contents

CHAPTER ONE

The Nature of the Female

Have you ever been confused with women's behavior? Specifically, why such beautiful women can be seen with what seems to be "very ordinary men"? Well, my fellow man, allow me to open your eyes. Whether you accept it or not, there is a level of dominance associated with the human male, much like in the animal kingdom. Our advantage as human males is the fact that we have a brain. With intelligence comes the ability to perceive, to change, to analyze our behavior. Let's agree that your existence as a man in today's world is a civilized one, but the fact remains we all want to attract women in a very basic, instinctive way. Moving forward, let us come to an understanding about one important general truth that effects you: You will never achieve your full potential for attracting the opposite sex unless you come to an understanding of your own behavior, your own position, your own weaknesses. The foundation of your success rests on this ability. Look in the mirror, be brutally honest with yourself, and this book will be the best investment you have ever made. You will gain a new sense of power and control in all social environments. Once you understand "why" you are who you are, you begin the process of moving up the chain to become a more dominant male.

The first thing you must do for yourself is wipe the slate clean. The evolution of your own behavior, up to this point, has been forged through your environment, your experiences, the observation of your parents' interaction, and many other factors. Who you are now is likely to be fine in the grand scheme of fitting in with what society calls "normal" or "average". The purpose of this book is to show you why you are where you are on the social scale with the Carrera

Dominance Principles and other behaviors you may have been unaware of most of your life. It is necessary for you to free up your mind and look inside. Forget what you've been told about "pick-up" lines and the use of language. If you have been reading some of the crap in bookstores everywhere about the "the right line", or "the rap that works", then you have some de-programming to do, my friend. My intent is to bring out the real you, not an actor in portrayal. I am going to open your eyes to the basics of human behavior and, believe or not, your unrealized ability to attract the opposite sex without saying a word. Intrigued? You should be. All I ask is that you approach this with an open mind and a willingness to learn as much as you can about human behavior. I want you to come to an understanding of your own behavior. I want you to be successful. Not just with the opposite sex, but with your life in general. At this moment, you exist in a comfort zone that is expandable. I am here to expand it for you. You are here because you have the desire to improve your standing in life, and that is admirable. However, you must be willing to venture out, absorb, and work on positive changes in your own behavior. If you are looking for a quick-fix approach to getting laid more often, then you have missed my point entirely and you have wasted your money. There is some effort and discipline required of you in your transformation. In addition, I ask that you be brutally honest with yourself in your analysis of who and where you are now. Keep these two concepts in mind as you read on. Let us begin.

CHAPTER TWO

Women- What's their Motivation?

To understand the behavior of women, we have to strip away all modern influences and understand a basic human instinct. Survival. It is in the best interest for a woman to choose a strong, dominant male to guarantee the survival of her offspring. That's it. Women are selective in their behavior because they have to be. Without consciously knowing their criteria for choice, they are pre-determined to select a strong mate. This guarantees that her own children will be strong and prosperous. Throughout our evolution, nothing has changed. Their sexual choices are guarded for this reason alone. In the early days of our history as humans, think of how tough it was to raise a child. It was critical that women find a mate offering strength and security for their offspring. Today, though women's choices are less life threatening, they still have advanced sensory skills when observing male behavior. Some they are conciously aware of, and some they are not. Think of women as having a sense of radar when reading a man's behavior. This ability is so critical for women, that this talent is highly evolved. That's why memorizing introductory lines and learning to say the right things to a woman have such a low success rate. Language on it's own is really a lazy man's attempt to get something for nothing. Wouldn't you agree? With this concept in mind, start to identify with all women. How do they choose a man? It's really very simple. Men are categorized according to their level of dominance, like the business world of today, with levels of power and dominance dependent on talents and abilities. Obviously, power itself is an attraction, but the spectrum of behavior that women observe goes far beyond this. As you read and absorb, keep in mind that dominance is a perception. It's a read on men, like a dolphin using sonar. Anyone can appear to be someone they are not, but the results will only be temporary. You are about to discover how to make permanent changes in your own behavior. Changes that will open all the doors that never seemed to open for you in the past.

In today's modern and civilized world, women have their hands full. What I mean here is that perceptions of men are often layered with false trappings. Case in point, a very wealthy man can be dominant in the sense that he has competed and won in the competitive business world, but without other dominant traits, the foundation is still weak. Don't misunderstand this. There are some women attracted by the single dimension of power or achievement coupled with nothing else, but the percentages of a sustained attraction are low and the motivations are not sincere. The problem that exists now, specifically in America, is that much of the perceived dominance, be it male or female, is related to financial success. What about the well balanced, intelligent man with a healthy self image and a passion for life that extends beyond the material trappings? The real truth is that character, morals, and behavior reflecting care and love is more cherished by the really beautiful women, if you catch my drift. It is true that many women "sell out", opting for simply the financially secure world of a man that offers little chance of being a true life partner. My advice here is not to sell out. Sharpen your instincts through the study of your own behavior and the light will start to shine on you, brother. You will start to see and understand what is really important in this world. We are all animals in a world where our instincts are no longer sharp. Your goal by reading this book is to sharpen your senses and see everyone as they really are. Once you recognize the true levels of dominance in the society of man, your own position becomes apparent. You have to know where you stand now if you are going to make positive changes.

Now, let's look at women's perceptions of the male personality and why "Mr. Personality" has become the myth it is.

CHAPTER THREE

Personality or Not

Before I begin, I have to acknowledge the role personality plays in attracting women. Personality, on its own, is worthless. That is, your persona as a man has no value unless it is exposed and used in ways that can offer women a pleasant snapshot of what it's like to be in your company. Let's look at the basic introvert-extrovert model. In Psychiatry 101, we are divided into two groups - the outgoing, gregarious, people-person and the quiet, introspective, man who is more comfortable with "things" than with people. Truth is, only an extreme few are pure extroverts or introverts. We all have traits that give us a blend, with tendencies toward one side or the other. If you are shy and reclusive, it by no means is an indication that you will fail in your attempts to be alluring to women. Just as being an animated, extreme extrovert is not a guarantee for success with women. That's why we de-emphasize the spoken word. The highly verbal male is perceived by men as having more potential to succeed with women. But this perception is not shared by most women. Most communication, especially between men and women, is non-verbal. Some say 80-20. It doesn't matter. Fact is, the shy, quiet male can reach the same level of success as the outgoing male. I'm not saying words are meaningless. We all speak thousands of words each day, but for the purpose of impression and seduction, very few words are needed. The most common mistake men make in the presence of women is what I call "throwing up" on them, meaning, filling up all dead time with what you think is important; information about you, anecdotes that involve you and how the world effects you. Get the idea? The idea is to get out of the "me" mode and ask questions that get her talking about her wants, her desires, and the things that she is passionate about. Every conversation is led by the one asking the questions. If she is doing most of the talking because you are asking most of the questions, chances are you're date is right on track. Your goal, however, as a dominant male, is to outwardly show your comfort with women, relax them in a way that makes them desire your company. Remember, most conversation is meaningless. Stop using conversation to fill dead time when you are with a woman. It shows lack of comfort. It is imperative that all neurotic thoughts and behaviors be eliminated from your speech and your body language. In other words, relax and be yourself already!

Though it is widely understood that most women are audible rather than visual, it means they get turned on more by language than by the sight of a chiseled male physique. Not just any language. I'm talking about specific language designed to seduce and create imagery. But that's another agenda, and you need to see where you stand in the pecking order before you begin your understanding of language. Most of us are blessed with a few personality traits that we have learned to exploit from an early age. Please understand that your goal here is not to change yourself. It is to take the positive attributes you possess now and expand them. Understand that your personality, unless you're Charles Manson, is just fine and you do not need to magnify it. If you are quiet, that's fine. If you are a talker, that's fine too. It's all in your attitude, your confidence, the way you carry yourself in social situations, and your ability to communicate on a one-to-one basis that determine your success with women. So what about your personality? Don't fret, my friend, I can almost guarantee you that there are many women out there that will love you the way you are. Most of us hit the wall in our search simply because we can't identify good chemistry when we find it. Look at personality simply as a fingerprint of character traits. In the conscious world, women want men with 'personality', but what are they really saying in all those Cosmo polls on the selection criteria for a good man? They want a match to their own personality! But let's not stop here. At the subconscious level, attraction is actually based on your physical appearance paired with your mojo, or personal 'aura' as it were. By this I mean your appearance and behavior reflecting your strength. You are, in fact, advertising your position as the best choice to guarantee that her offspring will be strong and prosperous. It's that radar at work again, and it's influence on her desire for you is critical to her. So critical in fact, that personality is secondary to her perception of you. After all, when you first meet a woman, can she really know the full spectrum of your character traits and make any judgement on your personality? Of course not. But this reading she gets, though very subtle, is the magnet that beckons her to approach and find out what you are about. In many ways, there is overt curiosity on her part, but still no real understanding of why she is intrigued by you. So, as for your personality, it does play a role, but understand now that this role is secondary to the primal selection process that she is using to evaluate you even before you explore each other's character traits. Strength and dominance are truly perceptions, and if you appear weak, or lacking in confidence, it won't matter what kind of personality you have.

We talked about the introvert-extrovert label for identifying personality, but where does the dominant male fall in this labeling process? Usually, it's somewhere in the middle. Fact is, most of us are not "pure" extroverts or introverts, but combinations of the two. Your combination determines which side you tend to lean to, and most of us move from side to side on this scale depending on mood, social setting, and personal levels of confidence for that moment in time. The tricky part to maintaining the role of a dominant male is not to be one or the other, but to permanently capture the level of confidence that exists inside you that surfaces only on occasion. How do you do that? Easy, my aspiring male. You first identify it. In other words, understand who you really are. Then, you make a conscious effort to change for the better.

CHAPTER FOUR

Are you an Introvert or an Extrovert?

The introvert/extrovert paradigm was first formally introduced by the famous Carl Jung, the explorer of the "Collective Unconscious" and a former student of the equally famous father of pychotherapy, Sigmund Freud. Most people are neither an extreme pure introvert or extravert. But it really does help to know where you are on the scale. The following questions are what is called 'forced choice'. In other words, you must pick the answer that most suits you:

You:

COLUMN E	COLUMN I
1) Value your social life	Value time to yourself
2) Tend to draw energy from a social gathering	Need to be by yourself to recharge your batteries
3) People are generally easy to read	Still waters run deep
4) Tend to offer your opinions quickly	Tend to hold back
5) You are the life of the party	You tend to withdraw
6) Being in a crowd energizes you	Being in a crowd drains you
7) You have many friends	You have a few <u>close</u> friends
8) Value stimulation	Value tranquility

The Extrovert

If you scored more selections in column 'E' then you are probably an extravert. You tend to be an open, talkative and relatively 'on the surface' or easy to read. You need interactions with people every day to keep 'your batteries charged. Sometimes you are annoyed with yourself because of a tendency to 'speak without thinking.'

The Introvert

If you scored more in the 'I' column then you tend to come across in public as quiet, reserved and sometimes shy. Even though you may desire social interaction, you really do need more peace and privacy than most people. You are more likely to think without speaking. And with you, "Still waters run deep."

CHAPTER FIVE

The Carrera Principles of Dominance

I know what you've been asking yourself as you read. What makes a man dominant? What is it about our behavior that draws women in like moths to a light? Or more importantly, what makes a man appear to be dominant or desirable? Is it possible to change my behavior so that I can become dominant? These questions require some explaining, but the simple answer to the last question is 'yes'. Let's look at what real dominance is.

Now, let's strip away our cultured upbringing and look at the core of human social behavior in men. In any gathering involving single people, you will see male behaviors at play. Some tend to "show off", that is, put on a show for the ladies. Some are quiet and subdued, perhaps uncomfortable in this setting. A few may even be threatened by what they perceive as competition. Others are gregarious and extroverted by nature, and may have no genuine interest in their behavior or their ability to attract women. In this setting, the truly dominant male is easy to spot. He's not there to put on a show. His attitude is "I don't have to". This man is confident, has great awareness and self-control, but does not overplay his hand. He's more than likely not the most attractive male in the room, either. Yet, to women, he is perceived as handsome, even curiously sexy. So who is this guy? He is the one who looks comfortable in this setting. He makes everyone, even men, feel comfortable in his presence. He makes eye contact, and does not appear to be distracted. He advertises his 'approachability'. His appearance gets notice not because of dashing looks, but his ability to display total confidence. His attire is usually going to be just a notch above the typical wear for the occasion. Most women in the room feel comfortable in his presence, and this comfort level precedes their attraction to him, which tends to grow with their own comfort level. When he speaks, he is deliberate, friendly, confident, and attentive. Think about how this behavior applies to your own. We have all been in a setting where we stress about what to say next or how to "act" in front a beautiful woman. What typically happens? Well, for most men, you feel like you "blew it" because you didn't appear intelligent or sexy enough in your actions and language. Perhaps it was because you were, in fact, acting, which in itself is very discomforting. The end result is failure, simply because you failed to make her feel comfortable in your presence. Sure, if George Clooney or Robert Redford were nervous, uneasy people in public, women would still be attracted to them. But the number of women will decrease dramatically. A comfort level must exist before real sexual energy can flow between you and her. So there it is. All you have to do is become more approachable. See how easy it is. But how? How do you become a truly dominant, approachable male that most women desire? Simple. You have to display the traits of a truly dominant male. It's not necessary to have a chiseled physique, drive a Porche, or strut around in five hundred dollar suits to be perceived as dominant. True, physical appeal, hygiene, and style of dress play a role, but these are common sense issues that are cut and dry and easy to improve upon, as you will discover later in this book. At this point, I'm assuming you are making an effort in this area to coincide with your new understanding and willingness to consciously practice your new "attitude".

So who is this ultimate man and what makes him so desired? The best way to explain this hierarchy is to reveal the Carrera Principle of Dominance. In it's developmental stages, the Carrera principles evolved over behavior studies ranging from five to twenty five years. Over one hundred highly successful and dominant men were studied, or monitored, with intent to discover successful behavorial traits. The common behaviors of these men were suprising and promising. Why? Well, a few common myths about what makes a ladies man a ladies man were broken, so to speak. Mainly, that outspoken, highly extroverted friend (everyone knows one) you think is desired by most women is in fact not at the top. Let's begin our discovery of who holds the top spot and how the scale trickles down the food chain. As you read, think about where you fall on the chart and why.

THE BALANCED DOMINANT MALE

This is the man at the top of his game and the top of the heap. By balanced, I mean he straddles the middle of the introvert/ extrovert model. Men who are balanced by nature are more keen to their own behavior and will "catch" themselves if obsessive or compulsive behavior starts to take over. A BALANCED MALE IS ALWAYS COMFORTABLE BEING WHO HE IS. Always comfortable and in control, this truly dominant man exudes an inner confidence instead of an outward bravado. He displays power but rarely exercises it. He understands control, and has a sense of humility and humor. His superior skills (in other words, why he attracts the ladies), is his confidence in all social and personal situations, and his ability to make almost all women feel comfortable in his presence. He has virtually no issues with handling nervous energy. Contrary to popular belief, he is not typically a heavy-handed talker, but he is an effective communicator with a developed talent for being personable. He almost always appears relaxed and attentive, with eyes that make and hold contact with a woman rather than dart about the room. This attentive and non-distractive quality is an asset in any social situation. He projects friendliness in his speech and body language to men and women alike, but, most of all, he does not strut his stuff for the ladies. After all, there is no need to perform or "show off" if you are already at the top. He knows that in a crowded nightclub, for example, women will scan the horizon and intently observe the behavior of the men around them. Of course, the flashy, loud, overtly friendly male will draw immediate attention. But the dominant male can command constant attention and will typically arouse the curiosity of most women. Feeling no need to perform means there is no need to compete, therefore, he makes no threatening moves and will never acknowledge the 'games' that take place between competing males. As the dominant male, he is keenly aware of his surroundings and how to read female behavior, and, once eye contact is made, looking women directly in the eye, smiling, and just being approachable is all that is needed to generate attraction.

THE DOMINANT EXTROVERT

This man takes the silver medal. He's outgoing, socially confident, and at ease with most people and places. He's the gregarious one at parties and becomes energized when he's around people in general. He will exercise power on occasion, and will often use an advanced sense of humor to soften or create comfort within a social setting. Most women desire him, but some don't. Though he is perceived as dominant, he may appear to be a little too arrogant, or perhaps not a good listener. The perception of men who come on strong is that this aggressive, overt behavior is a result of some form of insecurity. That is a possibility, but he still holds the second highest position of dominance. He feels no need to perform or show off for the ladies. He's just friendly by nature. There are occasional "bad boy" traits associated with these men, but it's usually a small part of his behavioral model. If he has the ability to empathize with women, it will certainly move him up the scale, but still short of the true balanced dominant.

THE DOMINANT INTROVERT

By his nature, the dominant introvert is the "strong, silent type". This was the biggest surprise in our behavorial studies, because men of few words are not typically associated with the passionate, womanizing gigolo. He may be somewhat uncomfortable in many social settings, but he owns a strong sense of self, and rarely appears outwardly nervous or fidgety. He attracts women with his quiet confidence in a way that mystery intrigues us all. He is usually approachable and is perceived as a man who will focus on one women with an intent to satisfy or please. Though quiet by nature, he has no trouble "turning it up a notch" if he feels the need. Again, because he is dominant, there is no desire to perform or change his behavior in order to be noticed by women. In other words, he is himself - no acting here. Often, this man has some of the "bad boy" anti-authority quality in his makeup, and many women are drawn to this type of attitude.

His "quiet confidence" has an inert appeal to most women. In addition, there is an interesting sexual discovery about the quiet, or shy, dominant male. Most women perceive them as being above average lovers. This is based on their ability to focus, to listen, and to empathize with nearly all women.

IF YOU FEEL THE NEED TO "PERFORM" FOR WOMEN, YOU ARE NOT A TRUE DOMINANT MALE.

THE BALANCED PERFORMER

This is the most common category in that most adult single men exist at this level. Most of us, when confronted with women in a social setting, do not feel completely comfortable with being ourselves and tend to "act" in a fashion that we feel will get us noticed. Sound familiar? This balanced performer is right there in the middle, with only slight introvert or extrovert qualities. What keeps this man from rising to a dominant level is confidence and understanding. Remember, confidence creates comfort, and comfort creates appeal to women in your presence. He spends too much time "acting" because he feels women will not find his true nature to be sexual or alluring enough. Not being yourself causes stress and visible stress is not sexy. In addition, when you perform, you must focus on your next line, just like any other actor. Problem here is that when you act, you don't listen, so even if you think of a clever question, you won't hear the answer because you're too busy concentrating on what to say next. Sound familiar? This lack of understanding women or listening hurts your effort to learn. You can't draw anyone in with language if you fail to become a good listener.

THE EXTROVERT PERFORMER

Slightly less common, this man is your basic outgoing, friendly guy with a keen awareness of most women in his presence. He is talkative in a social setting, and will often be the loudest and most animated among a group of men. Being more extroverted, he does not feel the level of stress the balanced performer does(not a lot of acting here), but there is some. Again, stress stems from lack of confidence, and though he seems confident socially, he has some hidden fears about being alone with a woman or having sincere one-on-one chit chat with a new aquaintance. Again, his discomfort translates to some nervous and fidgety behavior, but only in moderation. As we go down the scale of dominance, can you spot a common denominator?

THE INTROVERT PERFORMER

This man has the ability to relax in private, but will either close up completely in public or become a pure performer, meaning he is rarely himself in a social situation. He may be quiet and shy, and feels that these attributes are undesirable for women. His stress level is the greatest of the performers. Don't misread me here though. I'm still talking about a man with enough confidence to attract some women. Remember what I said earlier about shyness. It can definitely work for you with many women. The key to moving up to the Balanced Performer's level is learning to be comfortable with yourself and understand that your personality is not a bad one. There is no need to cover up, to perform, to show off, to impress.

Hell, it's very stressful to play-act most of the time you're in the presence of women. You should never equate shyness with weakness. There is no correlation. If you lean toward being quiet and reserved, use it to your advantage.

THE PASSIVE MALE

The passive male represents a moderate amount of men in our society. Whether introvert, extrovert, socially adept or socially shy, this man is low on the scale because he is low in self-belief. Typically, this man thinks of himself as non-sexual and will probably have a repressed libido due to self-loathing or any other factor that contributes to low self esteem. Men who are more than forty pounds overweight and/or practice poor personal hygiene would be part of this group. When a passive male spots an attractive women socially, he will always be uncomfortable and will feel that even moderately pretty girls are way out of his league. You may recognize this type as you scroll through your rolodex of acqaintences. Without a large dose of personal confidence, this man will always fail to appeal.

THE RECESSIVE MALE

Not much to say here. Here is a man with no confidence, poor habits(exercise, dress, hygiene, etc.), and very non-sexual in behavior. He will often have nervous habits, phobias regarding people and public places, and lean more to the introverted side on the personality scale. For some reason, this man takes no initiative to improve his condition(like purchasing this book for example). He may actually have potential to advance at least a few steps, but he simply does not care to put forth the effort. Enough said here. Let's move on.

CHAPTER SIX

Becoming the Dominant Male

Before we get into the talents and traits of dominant men, let's get the obvious, physical part out of the way. You don't have to be one of the beautiful people. Most dominant men start out as the average Joe, but make the effort to become more appealing. What I am talking about here is dress, hygiene, hairstyle, you know- physical appearance. It would be easy for me to advise you on improving your looks, but diet, exercise, and dressing in fashion are common sense issues and you should already know what to do here. If you need advice on what to eat and how to exercise, just pick up a copy of Men's Health magazine. One subscription will cover most of what you need. What I will tell you is that you, in your transformation to dominance, need to know what a dominant man looks like. First of all, he is not overweight or out of condition. It would be difficult to maintain any kind of status once you are thirty pounds overweight, so keep your weight under control. Second, dominant men dress well. Even with a bodybuilder's physique, most dominant men will play it down, whereas the performing sub-dominants will go for the tight clothing and "look at me" approach. Make your clothes fit well and dress slightly above the average if you really want to get noticed. Dominant men are well groomed. This attribute speaks for itself. If you need tips on grooming, this book won't be worth squat to you, because you haven't left ground zero yet. Anyway, I think you get the picture. Your goal here is simply to be pleasing to the women's eye. No big secret given away here. Your goal, in appearance, is to look above average. That's it. No plastic surgery, no bulging biceps, no deep, dark tan. Use common sense and do what you know is right for your appearance to improve. The term "balance" comes into play again. An obsession with the physical is perceived as a weakness by women. Too much attention on you translates to less on them. Anyway, I digress, and there are important behavior issues that need to be covered that are not so obvious. The best news I can give you regarding your own status is that growth is achievable. The Carrera study reveals that most men, as they age, do move up the scale. We're talking age twenty to forty, but even men in their fifties have advanced up the scale dramatically. Almost all teenage boys begin as awkward or performing males. Remember your own development and you will identify. The common denominator for men who advance dramatically (more than two levels) is an ability to self-analyze, and a strong desire to change weaknesses in their current behavior.

Now that you have a tangible scale of dominance to work with, you have the ladder in your sight and the effort to climb must come from you. I know you see yourself somewhere on this scale, and if you are honest with your evaluation, you have just completed the first step. Fear not, however, if you are lower on the scale than you anticipated. The good news is that we all have the capacity to improve in many ways. Never underestimate the power of your mind. I guarantee that at this moment in time, you are just scratching the surface. Like I said before, the men at the top possess many common denominators. Confidence is one, but there are other traits that you can build on that will move you up the scale.

Using the Carrera principles derived from all the successful men in the group, we've discovered several common traits that can take you into the stratosphere of dominance should you decide to apply them. All dominant men are in possession of five basic personality traits or "talents", even though some of these talents may be minor in existence. They are as follows:

1. CONFIDENCE. Not the cocky arrogant way they carry themselves or outward self confidence. This confidence is more internal. It makes them approachable. They are relaxed and poised in public. Dominant men use it to put a woman's guard down, so to speak. They create a level of comfort and security where anyone (men and women) will relax

and be themselves in their presence. For a woman, this in itself generates attraction. It is human nature to gravitate towards comfort, even when its provided by a man in mixed company. What women perceive as power is in fact social confidence on his part. Whether fantasy or real behavior, power perceived is power achieved. Fact: Truly dominant men never "act" or pretend to be someone else. They actually like who they are, and their level of comfort in all social situations is testimony. Their comfort is transferable in all social situations. Women feel at ease with them because dominant men are at ease with themselves, and women perceive this comfort as a great inner confidence.

YOUR NEW GOAL: STOP ROLE PLAYING AND BE YOURSELF.

2. EMPATHY. What I mean here is, the dominant man understands and relates to the women in his presence, and because of this, he is always perceived as personable and attentive. He is a champion listener

and coupled with the fact that he generates such a level of comfort, he can sit down and have a chat with any woman, be it Miss America or the girl next door. Fact is, everyone loves to talk about themselves, and women find inquisitive men very endearing. Catch my drift? So develop the skill of putting yourself in her shoes and stop simply reacting to her attitude. Align yourself with her and you can take her in any direction.

GOAL: LEAD YOUR CONVERSATIONS BY ASK-ING QUESTIONS AND LEARN TO BECOME A BETTER LISTENER.

3. FRIENDS FIRST, THEN LOVERS. (Expanding beyond the sexual). This talent is crucial in meeting a woman for the first time. Though sexual energy may flow upon initial meeting and there is lust coming from both sides, dominant men will often practice the age old art of just being friendly first. This phase of warming up with a woman may last two hours or two days, but if the relationship is to progress beyond a one night stand, the friend part has to come first.

Very basic, almost childlike friendliness, is essential to the success of any beginning relationship. Think of your youth and how you made friends in the schoolyard. It was all very innocent and childlike. Having a healthy sense of humor won't hurt, either. I'm not talking one liners, but a sense of what is funny and the ability to make a woman laugh. Think of the innocence of simply "playing" with a friend. Bring out her inner child with friendship and laughter, and you definitely have her attention and capture her imagination. Here's a universal truth: Women will admire and desire the man who can make them laugh and bring out the child in them.

GOAL: MAKE THE EFFORT TO GAIN A FEMALE FRIEND EVEN IF SEX IS NOT THE END RESULT.

4. HUMILITY. In simple terms, the self effacing ability we all have to laugh at ourselves and resist our temptation to blow our own horn. Think of the flashy dressing, Corvette driving, thick gold chain

wearing loudmouth that throws himself at women with exclamations of his own greatness. This ain't him. This dominant form of behavior is hard to maintain (we all love to brag), but this effort in control is well worth it. Women love to discover positive things about you that don't come from you. Understand? Learn to humanize yourself in the presence of women. Admitting to a weakness or flaw in your own character creates an alignment with her, like two people moving in the same direction. Why? Simple. All humans have flaws. She knew that before meeting you. To expose yourself in that way is an invitation into your emotional world, and few women will turn that down. Like a secret between friends, you create a "me and you against the world" alliance, and the more secrets you share with her, the closer she will feel to you. Trying to be Superman all the time is exhausting. Learn to show at least a few of your weaknesses and be willing to give up a few secrets along the way.

GOAL: CONTROL THE URGE TO BRAG AND
HUMANIZE YOURSELF IN HER EYES.

5. DESIRE/PASSION. The desire to learn and grow
and a desire for life. Even the most dominant of men
know they have weaknesses they must overcome
through learning. We all do. Dominant men tend to
be students of human nature. All thriving, successful
men (and women) have this trait engrained in them.
This works in direct relation to that other important
skill, listening. When you stop learning, you stagnate,
and as a dominant man you should always seek out
that what makes you grow. Don't just watch the
behavior of other men. Study it. You need to become
a student again. Behavior of dominant men observed
will become behavior applied. This step is so critical
that without it you will get nowhere. Desire equates
to hunger, and a hunger for life breeds a passion
that is noticeable to most women, and, believe me,
women find passionate men very appealing.

GOAL: OPEN YOUR MIND AND DECIDE YOU WANT TO IMPROVE, THEN TAKE STEPS TO INCREASE YOUR LEVEL OF PASSION.

See how easy it is attract women? All you have to do is make these five characteristics part of your own character makeup. Well, sorry, my gigolo wanna be, there is one part to this plan that has a catch. Fact is, number five comes first. You have to do two things on your own before anything can happen. First, you have to make a conscious decision that you will get off your butt and give it your best effort. Second, you have to practice, then practice some more, then again, and again, and again...I think you get my drift. In reality, the value of this book is in your hands. It can be worth nothing (if you were expecting a step-by-step guide on how to get laid), or it could be priceless should you decide you want to reach your potential as a man.

All male -female relationships have some or all of these common traits. I know what you are probably thinking at this point. What about the art of seduction? Well, the combination or your desire skills and your empathy skills contribute to your own ability to seduce. Seduction, in it's truest form, is the use of verbal and non-verbal communication to increase the chances of your partner's sexual arousal. When the attraction already exists, arousal then becomes a natural behavior. In other words, there is a before and after where attraction comes first.

You're new awareness of women and their nature should enhance your ability to communicate and to seduce. Women are audible by nature, so they do love the sound of a soothing male voice. But it does not stop there. You have to be effective in your language, which means using your imagination, being creative, and talking sexy or dirty, whichever she prefers. Now that more women than ever have gained a new freedom in the sexual arena, and openly admit their desire and pleasure to others, it makes your effort easier. It's acceptable to ask her what she likes to hear or feel. Use common sense here. Seduction is so much easier than you think it is once you consciously practice it. Remember, practice will eventually become instinct, and once you know exactly how to achieve the end result you desire, your confidence level jumps to the superman level.

Eventually, if you are talented and imaginative in your own efforts, you should feel as though you can seduce most of the single women you meet.

Now, regarding the five traits I mentioned, let's come to another understanding. All highly successful men (In life and love) have these traits in various combinations. Think of it as a personality fingerprint, with no two men being alike. At this moment, you may have most or even all of these traits, but never before have you consciously tried to expand them.

The most important single step you must take on this new road is that of control. Specifically, controlling the urge to perform. You are not a peacock with colorful plumage, you are a man. Fight that urge to 'act' or 'show off' because it may attract the eye of a cute blonde. True dominance needs no performance. So stop performing, and learn to be genuine. I confess, this is not an easy urge to control, but you must, and in the process, your own personal growth will take place. With any change there is initially resistance – that's your nature. We all put up a resistance to change, even if it's positive change. There is a part of your persona that has to be laid to rest in order for new behaviors to take hold. As difficult as it may seem at first, you must now venture into new territory. At this moment in your life I can safely assume that you thrive in a comfort zone created solely by your own mind. It's time for you to expand. It's time for you to recognize your own strengths and weaknesses, and alter old patterns of behavior that prevent you from reaching your potential.

CHAPTER SEVEN

Overcoming Fear

Now were getting down to the nitty gritty. Why doesn't everyone grow and expand throughout their lifetime and improve with age? The fact is, we(and yes, you too) are afraid of change. I'm here to tell you that fear is your enemy and for all practical purposes, only exists in your mind. Let me explain it this way. You're at a dance, you spot a pretty girl, make eye contact, and yet, you hold back on your effort to just walk across a room and ask her to dance. Plain and simple, this is the fear of rejection. Even the most powerful and intelligent of all men have levels of this fear. Why? It's a by-product of our infancy. Sure, as babies and infants we were solely dependent on others for our well being - food, shelter, nuturing, etc., but that fear was real. Your fear is not. To be rejected as an infant could have severe consequences, but you are an adult now, and injury, even death, will not result from a mere rejection. The only thing that keeps you in your comfort zone is this phantom fear. You must intentionally leave your comfort zone, and you must do it often to grow. Do things that are socially uncomfortable to you. For example, initiating a conversation with a woman you have never met before. The first time you do it, it may seem uncomfortable, but once you've left your artificial cave enough, you become a natural at it. So my instruction to you is:

DO SOMETHING EVERY DAY THAT FORCES YOU TO LEAVE YOUR COMFORT ZONE.

It doesn't have to involve women. It just has to challenge you to go somewhere you have never gone before. Something as simple as smiling and making eye contact in a social situation where you typically don't could be the challenge. You know what you have to do. Challenge yourself. If you understand anything about fear and expanding your comfort zone, know this important law:

SUCCESS IN LIFE AND LOVE IS DIRECTLY PROPORTIONAL TO THE NUMBER OF TIMES YOU INTENTIONALLY LEAVE YOUR COMFORT ZONE.

Why is this so important? Because leaving your comfort level behind translates to personal growth. You can't become more empathetic or confident or humble in the eyes of women unless you do it intentionally. At first. What I mean is, through repetition, behavior does become engrained, and eventually, there is very little conscious thought given to the practice of the five talents I mentioned earlier. Think of your comfort zone as a circle. Every time you leave the circle, it expands, then contracts when you retreat inward. But here's the exciting part. It does not contract back to its original size. It has expanded, though by just a small amount, on a permanent basis. That is, in essence, the purpose of publishing the Carrera Theory of Behavior. It's a real guide to real human tendencies. If you gain just a small understanding of this behavior, your comfort zone will expand on a permanent basis. So you must go forth and practice. Practice making friends with women, practice empathizing, practice the art of humility, and keep your mind open. Make a checklist and set out to accomplish these behavioral changes in your everyday life. Make the effort. Practice on your weakest points first. Your new confidence will be the by-product of your new adventures.

CHAPTER EIGHT

Pro-active vs. Reactive

I need to touch on this school of thought regarding behavior before we can move on. It's important because it has a direct bearing on how fast you can progress, all other factors being the same. The pro-active/reactive label is used in identifying the origin of your speech and behavior. That is, the last time you spoke, was it in reaction to someone or something, or was it original in it's process? We all have combination personalities under this classification, but the more pro-active you can be, the better off you are. Why? Because it means you have a high level of self control. If you tend to react to others in a more impulsive, "speak without thinking" mode, it makes you more reactive. This does not make you a weaker person. A certain level of passion is associated with reactive people, and passion is a very positive attribute. The problem arises when you become too reactive, and most of your speech and levels of emotion are dictated by outside forces, instead of internally. The less you let other peoples' speech and behavior control your speech and behavior, the more dominant you become. You remain in control, and he who is in control always has the upper hand. So if you tend to react rather than plan your speech or behavior, you will need to beef up your effort to control yourself emotionally. Without it, you will always move laterally through life, but never upward. At the core of all behavior lies control. If control is lost, you have complete chaos, and you have probably experienced some form of chaos in your lifetime. If you really think about it, you are faced with only two things each and every day. What you can control and what you can't. Trouble is, we tend to spend too much of our daily reserves of energy on people or things we have no control of, yet stress over. Stress, like fear, is an irrational form of thought, but it can dominate your behavior if you let it. Stop stressing over what someone said or did or what other people might think if you say this or that or just generally worrying about anything out of your immediate control. Control what's in your domain to control, like your own thought process, what you eat, the clothes you wear, what you say, where you travel, etc.. Anything else you attempt to control will induce stress and doom you to constant frustration and despair. If there is one glaring common denominator in the personality makeup of dominant men, it is the fact that they are rarely out of control. In the Carrera studies, the dominant males had come to this understanding through their life experiences, usually early in life, but the difference between them and the lower level males was that it registered in their subconscious mind and influenced their future behavior. The correlation between dominance and pro-active men is staggering. All dominant men have high levels of self control. Of course, all performing males, or what I call sub-dominants, are more reactive and have less control. After all, isn't control associated with strength? You bet your ass, pal. In the professional sport of boxing, it is common knowledge that the man who loses his temper in the ring (No reference to Tyson, here) will forget all his training, stop thinking about his plan of attack, and start getting the everlovin' crap beat out of him. Why? Control. He is now in a much weaker state because his self-control took a back seat to his emotions, and without using your mind as the true instrument of control that it is, you will always be weak. Remember, women read this behavior, and to them, a man not in control is undesirable. There is a great internal confidence that comes with knowing that you are not at the mercy of your environment, so jump on this bandwagon immediately, and begin practicing the art of 'self control'. If you truly have a strong desire to become more pro-active, that is, working on your 'issues of control', then you can readily absorb and put to use the Carrera principles of behavior.

IF THE BEHAVIOR OF OTHERS DICTATE YOUR OWN BEHAVIOR AND ATTITUDE, YOU WILL ALWAYS BE A SLAVE TO THE REST OF THE WORLD.

Identifying Territorial Behavior

Again, let's look at the animal kingdom. We have all seen the males of a species fighting over the right for territory. After all, we (single men) are all in competition with each other for the attraction of women. Our culture and civilized upbringing makes it unacceptable to simply pummel your competition into submission. You must handle this fact of nature in a more subdued manner in your quest for dominance. Looking at the true model of dominance, understand that your own urges to compete must be controlled. To be threatened by another male is an admission on your part that you exist on his level, and his level is truly that of a performer. The best way to explain this is to look at an obvious scenario. In any social setting where there are multiple single women and men, men do become threatened, though their reaction through behavior and body language is much more subtle. Watch these behaviors as you enter this setting. The threatened males will react by positioning, posturing, and even aggressiveness in some cases. They may intercede between you and the most desirable females by simply blocking your view or entry into a space that is 'theirs'. They may become more animated in action and more verbal in order to distract and bring the attention of the females back to them. Other men who may be engaged in conversation or simply in the acceptable space of desired females, will often turn their back to you as they position themselves between you and their conquest. It's fascinating body language like this that is easy to spot, and as a dominant, you have already won because you are aware of it and your performer subdominant has no clue. The way you handle these 'threatened' males is easy. They are no threat to you. Your attitude and demeanor must project this in their presence. Believe me, the females are in tune to all this positioning and posturing by men. If you feel no threat, you will not, I repeat, not acknowledge threat. No matter how uncomfortable it may feel at first, you must intentionally invade their space because you belong anywhere you want to be as a self-proclaimed dominant. Be polite and friendly, but treat these men as though they are almost invisible to you. When you make eye contact with the females in mixed company, be direct, but be friendly and unassuming. Let the positioning, posturing, and aggressive or defensive behavior come from them, and though it's a very subtle, almost subconscious transition, suddenly, the females become intrigued by you simply by your actions and behavior. Words are hardly necessary, nor the beating of your chest. It's a pretty cool thing when you think about it. In your effort to stand out and be noticed by women, you now have the upper hand. You should know that just a small effort in self- control on your part goes a long way. The trick here is understanding and identifying competing males when you see this activity in front of you. Your behavior has to be modified to assume a social stance of dominance or you will just become another pathetic sheep following the herd to slaughter, so to speak. Stop thinking in terms of tradition and learned behavior. Be your own man. Stand out. Are you up to the task?

Be Desireless and Excellent

In the independent film, The Tao of Steve, an ordinary, somewhat overweight man has amazing success with women. What was his method? He stated it as,"To be desireless and excellent". Let's break this down word by word. What is this desireless-ness? Is this not a contradiction? Is not this whole book about obtaining something that we desire? Yes, it is a seeming contradiction and that is the Zen of it. Often, as illogical as it may seem, the surest route between points A and B is often not a straight line.

And in this context, that can mean that you should go to that bar for a drink, that you go to the coffee shop to read, that you join that coed volleyball team to play volleyball. Of course on some hopefully sublimated level you went to these places to meet women. However, if a degree of desirelessness is cultivated on your part, women will sense this. They will perceive that you are not actively pursuing them, they will be intrigued. They will feel your resistance and therefore your challenge.

Then it will be up to them if they pursue you or not.

Excellence.

Do something and do it well. However it must be something that can be displayed. This can be dancing, playing the guitar, tennis, just something that can be observed in some context. If you don't have this skill, then find something you have a proclivity for and develop it. As we said, the truest route between points A and B is often not a straight line.

Talk to Women

This can fall into the desire less category. Talk to any and all women. Forget your ultimate agenda. Your goal here is to expand. You have inside you, as we all do, the ability to be creative and imaginative in our communication with women. You will find that the more you open up to women, the more comfortable you are, and the more comfortable you become, the more creative and original you will be. As you venture out of your comfort zone more and more, your own 'style' will become evident, and everyone loves to converse with people who are original, imaginative, and unpredictable. Remember what word pictures do for women. Imagery is powerful and will capture anyone's attention. Learn to tell a short story, a funny anecdote, or a passage of personal experience in colorful ways. In other words, learn to paint word pictures. Empathy coupled with friendliness is at play here. Remember that all women have a little girl inside that longs for simple pleasures. Learn to tap into her inner child with visual language, and you can lead a woman anywhere. I know it's easier said than done, but creativity on your part is not something you can achieve through study. It has to occur through application. This means leaving your secure, private world and opening up to more women. Learn to conquer your fear of rejection, and you will find that you are rejected a lot less than you anticipated. Go forth and talk to any and all women when the opportunity arrives. You will find it fun, exciting, and it beats looking at your watch in disgust as you stand in line at the post office. As time passes, you will be surprised at how comfortable you become, and how approachable you are. Other women will also see that you are comfortable speaking to the opposite sex and this will make you more approachable. So, talk to women when the opportunity presents itself. To be seen with other women, of dating quality or not, is a good thing. And ultimately, if you have trouble talking to women, this is great practice for when the one you really want to talk to finally arrives. But when one arrives, how ready are you? Let's back up again and see. Remember, for someone to see value in you, it helps to see value in yourself, and if you are uncomfortable and uneasy in your communication with women, you are picked up on the 'radar' of women as having little value.

Mental Mastery

You must master your desires. In Eastern philosophy it was said," The most disciplined man is the most free". The meaning to derive here is to not be a slave to your passions and desires. It is OK to want to know someone better, but it is not OK to need them. If you feel you need them, you have lost control of your emotions. The rulers of your life are now either your passions, the person you think you need, or even both. Also, a sense of neediness is the close in-bred cousin of desperation. Desperation is the left-handed, red-headed, bastard step-son of fear. And my friend, fear has a stench that women, children, small dogs and even small, furry forest creatures can smell.

Go forward, as a real man, be co-dependent on no one,

but love in a way that has no conditions. Remember our discussion on control. So few people truly control their lives, and the shame of it is that we tend to look externally for solutions to our shortcomings. Start looking within, for it truly is 'Nobody's fault but yours' if you have failed to gain control of your life up to this point. So learn to be your own 'mental master'. Your mind is the single most important resource you have. Why not develop it?

Affirmations, imagery and self-hypnosis

When left alone, what do we think about? Or at least what kind of thoughts do we entertain? Just as a full eighty percent of our human communication is non-verbal when with people, a whopping ninety percent of our thoughts tend to be negative when we are left alone. The reasons for this are many: it can be from your very in-born temperament, it can be from your environment, it be from your present situation, or perhaps negative influences from your childhood. It can be from one thing, but usually it is just part of the human situation. So, if you are honest enough, and reflect, you will notice that when left alone, many thoughts are negative and they are often about fighting other people! Well my man, unless you are in a war, this is just wasted energy. Remember this,

The Mind is a Garden

You can not control everything in your life. How much we control things that happen to us are continually being debated by scientists and philosophers. However, you do have control of how you perceive and process events. But as with many things human, and for most of us, it is a learned skill. Then again, there is some evidence to support the idea, that even how we process negative or positive thoughts can influence our realities.

The Dimensions of the Mind

The human brain, as wonderfully complex as it is, will be broken down into three parts for the purpose of this

discussion. There is your **conscious mind**, your ***gatekeeper***
and your **subconscious mind**. Your **conscious mind** is the
part of your consciousness that you are most aware of. This
part of you navigates throughout the daily reality of your
life. It is your conscious awareness of yourself and your
surroundings. Let us liken this state of mind to **daylight**.
Now let us consider another part of your brain's function,
your *sub-conscious*. Since we are largely unaware of
it, let us call this state of mind, **nighttime**, or even **sleep
time**. In between these two minds is our gatekeeper. The
gatekeeper controls information that passes between these
two worlds. Now, since we are likening these two states
of mind to a length of time, we should, to be fair, equate
daytime or consciousness to the standard 12 hour day, and
subconsciousness or nighttime to a full year of darkness!
This is because, my friend, of the inherent power of your
own mind, your…

Subconsciousness.

Most of us have heard the saying," We only use 10% of our brains". What was meant by that?

Do you remember when you were in a recent conversation with someone and you paused to remember a detail to add to the conversation? You looked up, concentrated, let go, then it came to you. Who delivered the information?

Your subconscious.

Do you remember when you first started driving a car? You had to intensely concentrate on everything; your brake foot, your gas application, your turns, the street signs, etcetera and so forth. So, who drives your car now?

Your subconscious.

Housed within your brain, is a wonderful thing, that for lack of a better word, we will call it a computer. Your subconscious mind is continually working for your interests. However, it does have limitations, mainly in that it believes what you tell it. If you continually feed it information that you are a great person and deserve all good things, then the subconscious mind will continually work for you to make this a reality. If on the other hand, you had an uncaring parent or guardian tell you how worthless you were as a child, you may easily grow up with this seed implanted in your brain. This seed, over the years can and often does, grow into a big ugly tree; the branches and leaves spreading out through your life as: failed relationships, bad grades in school, not living up to your potential, overly blaming others for your misfortunes and being generally unhappy.

Your Defective Computer programming

If this reflects your life in any way, you must make the mental leap that it was not all externally caused. In other words, yes, let us allow the notion that your ex really was a bitch, and yes your old boss really was a tool. However, if you have low self-esteem, you will sub-consciously draw these people to you and unknowingly sabotage other good things and relationships that come your way. Now, let us consider the middle man. He lives in the twilight of our two minds of day and night, he is the

Gatekeeper.

The gatekeeper works closely with the conscious mind. It takes in information that you receive during the day and interprets it as either true or untrue. However, it also works with the subconscious part too. In other words, if someone, or yourself says, "You're a great person." Your gatekeeper may reject this information, thus not allowing this affirmation into your sub-consciousness. So, as you may see, the gatekeeper is like a filter, that lets in only certain, select information that the sub-consciousness will process. So, how do we change a lifetime of bad programming? Well the repetition that we previously mentioned is an excellent start. Over time, this will reap many benefits. However, you may also want to reprogram yourself in an even more basic manner to help your confidence and to nip any self-sabotage motivations in the bud. This leads us to,

Knowing Your World and Yourself

Digress again to the Eastern saying, " The most free man is the most disciplined man." Of course, this may be interpreted many ways. However, as it is in the context of mental mastery, it means that he who controls his thoughts is ahead of the game. Many Eastern aesthetes have practiced this mental mastery in the form of meditation. There are as many ways in which to meditate as there are religions. Some of the most hardcore techniques have to do with "emptying the mind," whereas the meditive practicioner literally trains himself to *not think thoughts* for a period of time. If you happen to think this is easy, I challenge you to set a five minute timer, close your eyes and do not think for those five minutes.

After you have failed miserably, please continue reading.

This is not a put-down of the Eastern tradition of mental mastery. It's just that Western man usually does not have the time to become a cloistered monk and live on a mountaintop while perfecting his mental processes. Western Man needs something a little more pragmatic, and dare I say, something a little quicker.

While some meditation exercises involve imagry and the contemplation of certain, specific ideas, there is another mental method that is more short-term and goal directed. And as in the Eastern tradition, it does require a work ethic in consistancy and effort. It is called hypnosis.

Hypnosis.

What it is not

Hypnosis, forever being dramatized by stage hypnotists, has many false allusions associated with it. A person under hypnosis is not truly asleep. A person under hypnosis will not commit crimes that they would not normally do. A person in a hypnotic state will not necessarily forget what happened to them in the hypnotic trance-state. Finally, hypnosis can change your life, but it is not likely to produce miracles. Hypnotizing yourself for basically non realistic goals is at best, a form of self-delusion and at worst, it is yet another form of self-sabotage.

Hypnosis

What it is

However, There are degrees of hypnotic induction. If you are heavily concentrating on a movie, along with the hallmarks of 'suspension of disbelief' or are concentrating on reading a novel, these concentrated states of mind are indeed low levels of hypnosis.

A person who is deeply under, is not really asleep, they only seem asleep in that they are tightly focused on one thing to the exclusion of the rest of the world. This is vitally important because it is like the difference between a flashlight beam likened to normal amounts of attention or concentration to likening a deep level of hypnosis to a laser. What's more, hypnosis is also like flying under the radar of the gatekeeper. Hypnosis does not ask the gatekeeper's approval, it simply bypasses him!

The mechanics of hypnosis

Hypnosis, formally introduced by Anton Messmer in the 1700s, has been written about profusely since that time. However, this is brought up to illustrate that with every book written about it, there are just as many opinions about it. Therefore, upon completion of this read, the reader is encouraged to further educate himself with other tomes on the subject.

That said, There are at least two stages in the hypnotic process. The first is vital to the success of the rest, it is called *clearing*.

Clearing is the exercise in which the subject enters into a state of utter relaxation and then extreme focus. The reason for this is that in our waking day world, we are constantly using our external senses to get through the day. By employing a relaxing exercise, you will eliminate the distractions of the day and at the same time practice and employ a self-discipline that is helpful for success in that it begins to direct the mind in a specific direction.

Once a person is relaxed or under, it is time for the

suggestions to be implanted. Most of these suggestions are usually in the form of affirmations. Affirmations are basically positive ideas or assertions that are designed for personal growth. But a warning, do not use negatives in your affirmations. They tend to confuse the issue. And a confused sub-conscious is not a good thing. For example:

Positive Affirmation> "Women find me attractive". (Good!)

Negative Affirmation> "Women don't find me repulsive". (Not so Good!)

Another note on suggestions. It is generally considered a good idea to make suggestions and affirmations a present-progressive idea. In other words, the emphasis is now and ongoing, not tomorrow. " Women find me attractive". The *now* is a definite implication here.

A self-hypnosis example

If you pay someone to hypnotize you, that is your prerogative. However, there is a school of thought that states that all hypnosis is self hypnosis in that a person *allows* a hypnotist to put them under.

But what works for each individual can be different and if you pursue this avenue of self-improvement, you need to travel that road and see what works best for you.

If a person were to go solo, this is one way:

Write a short script get a tape recorder and tape it. In your script, you will begin by instructing your body to relax bit by bit.

"My left leg is now fully relaxed."

"My right arm is totally limp."

"My neck is totally loose."

Once the entire body is taken care of, you may concentrate on your breathing and begin visualations.

"I am breathing in deeply to the count of four."

"One, two, three , four."

"I am breathing out a fine blue mist to the count of four."

"One, two, three, four."

When the whole body is covered, you may instruct yourself that you will be completely under by the count of ten:

"One, I am going into a deep, trance state."

"Two, I am going deeper into my mind, this will be a

good session." (Get the idea here?)

"Ten, I am now completely in a hypnotic state. I am completely under."

After your body is completely relaxed and focused, a subject may direct himself to a nice environment, like imagine yourself swinging in a hammock between two shade trees on top of a hill that's in the middle of a field with the sun out and white clouds skimming by. Get the picture? Make it as elaborate as you like.

Now, once you have relaxed your body and put yourself in a 'good place', it is time to feed your mind positive affirmations and suggestions. After this is accomplished. Do a reverse of the number game. For instance:

"I will count backward from ten. When I reach one, I will be fully awake.

"Ten, I am starting to wake up, this was an excellent session."

"Nine, I am now a much better person than I was before."

"Eight, I'm waking up now, I feel great." ,,,,

By the time you reach 'one', You instruct yourself to

wake up and to proceed with your better day.

Timed, a script may look like this:

5 minutes: Nice relaxing music of your choice.

5 minutes: Relaxing the body.

4 minutes: The count-down.

5 minutes: The happy place (real or imaginary).

5 minutes: The happy thoughts, (affirmations).

4 minutes: the count up to the number ten.

So, to recap the self-hypnosis exercise.

A session should not be hurried, it should last about thirty minutes as it takes time to reach the proper mental state. It is like exercise, if you do this, make a habit of it, say three to four times a week. If self hypnosis is not appealing to you, I suggest some simple meditation exercises. Meditation will help to clean up your thoughts, keep you focused, and give that healthy mental outlook you will need to work on yourself. You can find material on meditation on the net or in most bookstores in the self-help section.

Hypnosis and meditation are internal processes, and though they will strengthen your mind, it is ultimately your effort in 'getting out there' and being active that will pay off in big dividends. Be willing to venture into new social settings and open up to meeting new people. Your social experiences from this point forward should be absorbed as a study of all human nature.

On Advertising Self-Improvement

Here's yet another old saying, " Your friends want you to do well,, just not better than them." There's a lot of truth there guys. Some nosey types believe that if you keep secrets, then you are guilty of some crime and therefore are hiding something subversive. However, why is the 'right to privacy' imbedded in our country's constitution?

The reason? Refer back to the old saying.

Whenever you publically tell people about an exceptional endeavor that you are undertaking, you definitely run the risk of either overt or passive-aggressive sabotage from your friends, not to mention from aquaintances and other associates. So, self-help is your business and not the worlds'. If you feel someone could benefit from the help we are attempting to provide, then kindly direct them to our website.

CHAPTER NINE

A Snapshot of a Dominant Male

It's time now to look at some of this behavior through one case study that is typical enough for almost every male to identify with. Our subject, Jack, is a dominant introvert out on the town and ready to meet the challenges of the social scene. A noisy nightclub with live music is Jack's choice, and he intentionally relaxes his demeanor before entering. Once in, he can survey the performing males, and make smart decisions about any mutual attraction he may have with any of the single women. As a dominant, he is calm, focused, and friendly. Jack notices a girl, we'll call

Betty, sitting at the bar with a friend. She watches the band play and occasionally talks to her friend. But she is shy in this situation and Jack reads this, as there is little attempt on her part to make eye contact with any of the available males. Betty is pretty and is being noticed by several males, but seems slightly uncomfortable. Jack's priorities are to make eye contact with Betty, formally meet her, and make her feel at ease. When the noise level is low, Jack introduces himself, without any fancy rhetoric and simply states to Betty, "I hope you don't mind, but I just wanted to meet you". Jack's intent is to make a new friend and he does. He does not inhibit her space, nor take the assumption that he has her consent to "be with her" for the evening. Jack is asking questions to learn about Betty, and in a few minutes simply bows out with "Nice meeting you". Jack knows that if Betty is genuinely attracted to him, they will talk later(Note the confidence). Three important things were accomplished here. First, Jack left his comfort zone as an introvert initiating a first meeting. Second, while maintaining a relaxed, friendly attitude, he set a short term goal to simply "make a new friend". Finally, and most important of all, he was successful in his attempt to make her feel comfortable in his presence. Though Jack is in another part of the room, he makes eye contact with Betty with a smile, and, noting an opportunity for a first dance(always a slow dance), he can invite her to dance, literally gesturing to Betty from across the room as he moves towards her. Phase two for Jack is now to escalate Betty's comfort level, because a first slow dance between any two people can be reasonably uncomfortable. Jack intentionally relaxes Betty by stating his comfort level with her and again gets her talking about herself. Again, using humility, Jack's attitude is that of "privilege" and makes a complimentary statement or two while they dance. Jack's obvious intent in Betty's eyes, is that of interest, but Jack is careful not to make obvious sexual "come on" statements or be caught taking a sneak-peak at her framework, so to speak. If chemistry is to occur, it will either escalate or it won't, and any dominant male knows this. When they part ways, Jack asks politely , "Would it be all right if I called you?"(It's better than "Can I have your phone number?").

Obviously, Betty will accept a first date based on how comfortable she feels in Jack's presence and her attraction to him. Jack's objective is to learn more about Betty, and to resist the urge to brag and boast of himself. As Betty becomes more comfortable in Jack's presence, she will begin to become more inquisitive and Jack can disclose any positive attributes of himself in small doses of pleasant little surprises for Betty. Jack brought their bond to it's highest level by sharing a secret about what he considers a weakness that he needs to work on. Betty's interest was peaked, first because Jack was willing to open up emotionally, and second, because the "secret" was of a sexual nature. In essence, the secret was of a nature that is normal for male sexual behavior in our society, and Jack knew this beforehand. It also gave Betty a snapshot of just how passionate Jack is as a man. All this would intrigue virtually any female.

Please consider this case study as just a guideline and not a quick "how to" lesson on "sealing the deal". What I want you to learn here is a pattern of behavior. As a dominant, Jack is confident and relaxed with Betty. He constantly empathizes (listens intently) with her and definitely succeeded in developing a new friendship. Finally, his passion(desire) became obvious to Betty early in their dating relationship, and the fact that Jack resisted the urge to talk about himself or strut his stuff for Betty not only intrigued her, but his level of humility was just an additional lure of attraction. Be careful, however, in your own approach to meeting and dating women, not to take a "cookie cutter" approach. Just keep these five behavioral principles centered in your mind when you meet a woman. From this point forward, practice it, then purposely apply it as often as you can.

First encounters with women should be looked at with intrigue and suprise on your part. Be genuinely excited and it will show in your eyes, your facial expressions, and your body language. We all have our mood swings, our ups and downs in energy, but the trick is to take advantage of those times you feel a little extra confident. Jack, the dominant male in our first case study, is not much different from you. Fact is, he's no Valentino, but he's now a model dominant after years of intentionally modifying his own behavior. As I mentioned before, as a dominant he dresses a little above the pack with tailored, well fitting clothes that are in style, has meticulous grooming habits, and he carries himself with a quiet confidence. This may sound a little over the top, but the next time you enter a room of mixed company, before you hit the door, check your attitude and demeanor. Practice putting out that "Air of confidence" vibe. Say to yourself, "I can make any woman in this room smile and take her anywhere I wish". The mind is so awesomely powerful, yet many of us let it waste away. Always remember how powerful the human mind is.

Now, let's take a look at another recorded case study that started from the early days of evolution into dominance. It involves another dominant introvert, Don, who migrated into the dominant role over a period of only two years. His advancement is not uncommon for middle aged men following divorce or the ending of any close relationship. The first step in improving his behavior(and attitude) was brutally honest self-examination. Without even knowing the key elements you have just been exposed to, Don determined that he was indeed lacking in confidence, humility, and was essentially weak at making female friends. He knew too, that he needed to "let himself go" so to speak. By this I mean letting people know what he was feeling, and generally allowing his hunger for life to shine through. As men, we are taught at an early age to fight the urge to be too emotional, so many of us hold back our moments of sorrow or joy or even our contentment with those everyday pleasures. Anyway, Don had a grasp of his weakness, and without consciously knowing it, had set out to correct his path in life.

Don's physical appearance was above average to begin with, but he decided to take it up a notch. His lifestyle change included three weight training sessions per week and two aerobic sessions per week. Sounds like overkill, but each workout rarely lasted more than a half an hour. As an intelligent man, Don knew how to keep things in balance, and resisted the urge to become obsessive with appearance. Don has average looks, but the fact that he's now in the upper two percentile of all adult men regarding fitness and appearance makes his attraction to women much more "immediate". So we know he's got it together here, but what about his behavior? What did he do to jump start a social life that had women constantly calling him? How did he migrate from a "possible date this weekend" to "Out of the five women I know have a crush on me, who should I go out with this weekend?

First, let's look at confidence. For Don, it was a result of effort, discipline, and the expansion of his comfort zone. His changes in lifestyle now include exercise, improved nutrition, a strong desire to learn, and most importantly, disregarding those phantom fears we all have when it comes to rejection. Don's result was a dramatic increase in self confidence, of course. The ability to empathize was Don's biggest flaw in the early days of his efforts. He worked hard at becoming more attentive with the women he was meeting. Without knowing it, Don was "practicing" this ability. He just knew that to be attentive, to really listen, and to have recall of even small trivial things suddenly did not seem so trivial(especially to her). Now, the ability to empathize and be attentive to women is Don's strongest asset. His secret is what he calls "mental bullet points" that he registers for use at any point in the future. For example, on their first date, Don learned that Wendy had a love of white roses. She said it in a casual, non-emphatic way, but it still registered with Don. Four dates later, what do you think happened when Don showed up at her door with white roses?

Bullet points. Remember the simple pleasures and anything that makes her happy. Don also discovered, as you will too, that it's all right to ask certain questions. A few of his favorites are as follows:

What makes you smile inside?(Whatever it is, chances are it can be duplicated, arranged, delivered, etc.) What do you think makes a man sexy? (This is her telling you how she can be seduced, so listen) What's more important to you, a man with unbridled passion or a man who is responsible and dependable?(Most women want both, and you can be both of these men as a true dominant) What's the best birthday gift you ever received? (Find out what she really likes)

If you were stuck on a deserted Island for a month, who would you wish was there with you? Why? (You are beginning to unlock some of her deepest interests and desires, so pay attention).

Here is a simple rule that Don has followed for years. If you want to sell something (yourself) to someone, then ask what makes them buy. Very simple, but highly effective. Hence, the listening and learning skills were crucial to Don's success.

Though an ex-college athlete with talents in music and a vivid imagination, Don was content to focus on his dates without spewing out all his positive attributes. This holding back really helped. Humility of this kind attracts, not to mention the intrigue and mystery that goes with her discovery of you in small bits and pieces.

As a newly arrived dominant, Don knew if chemistry existed when he met and dated women. If there were sparks, he knew he could fan the flame, but he was careful to develop a bond with women before sex was involved. Again, without knowing it, he was making a new friend and creating an overwhelming desire on her part to associate with him.

With an increase in dating came an increase in the number of poor opportunities, and Don also learned from observation and listening that some women are doomed in almost any relationship because of who they are.

Relationships, Dating, and Common Myths

While you are on the road to male dominance, developing your observation skills will become critical. There are signposts along the way, and your new "street smarts" will guarantee that you make few mistakes. One of the pitfalls to your newfound popularity is that you do have more choices. It's a great problem to have, but you must become skilled at knowing the real agendas and motivations of all these new, interested women. As I mentioned earlier, most men are currently performers in some measure, and this behavior does lend itself to an occasional fatal attraction. Let me explain. Any new relationship that originates with performance behavior on your part tends to perpetuate more performance behavior because your lady friend now expects it. Somewhere in the Dogma of Male-Female relations, there is a myth that as a man, it's your job to entertain, to please, to be attentive, and to always be the leader. All relationships require a dual effort to succeed and honest behavior. Some of the crap women are fed in articles and books tell them to "act" a certain way in order to control or manipulate the man they seek. Telling anyone to act out of character is wrong, and if you took a woman out on a second date to a restaurant, according to the "dating rules", she should act distracted and disinterested so that you will chase her and call her with more intensity. The problem here is that this is intentional manipulation. If your date can't look you in the eye, or even admit that she would like to know more about you, why would you continue dating her? Put the shoe on your foot, now. If you acted disinterested and distracted, would you expect her to go out with you again? Look at the contradiction and hypocracy of this kind of advice. What they tell women is complete nonsense. Disingenuous behavior is the absolute worst way to begin a relationship. Forcing a man to respect women only works temporarily, and the irony of a relationship that begins this way is that women eventually lose respect for themselves after they realize that it began under false pretenses. If a man does not respect women, it can't be forced upon him. Ignorance is still ignorance. If you find women playing these games, and some will, simply ask them to explain their behavior in a curious, but diplomatic way. "I was just curious, you seemed a little distracted in the restaurant and even a little disinterested when I called. Can I ask you why you continue to see me? I'm confused." In other words, when a woman pretends, you need to be aware of it and have the ability to bring her back to the real world.

What makes the application of these five behavorial principles any different? Are we not telling you to "act" a certain way. Does it make you a hypocrite when you apply the five behaviorial principles?Good questions. The answer is no. Why? Well, because there are negative and positive influences on your behavior. All five traits are positive influences on you. Intentionally striving to improve your behavior through acting or modification is fine, and anyone who does this(male or female) should be complimented. Deceit, however, comes in all forms. It is true that your new information can be used as a catalyst to satisfy desires for multiple sex partners, with the conquest of "sealing the deal" being your final objective. That doesn't make the principles wrong. It means your agenda is flawed, or morally corrupt, so to speak. The difference between you and a con man is that your final agenda is that of happiness and you should truly want your partner to be happy too. We all want to find the life partner we know is out there. What you need to do is learn "how" to search and have some kind of understanding about human nature so you can spot the good and the bad.

Unless you want to live with daily frustration levels climbing higher and higher, you must avoid women who are "relationship passive", meaning, they take little or no initiative to please you. These high maintenance ladies wear you out simply because they are ignorant of the condition of their own behavior. Case in point. An extremely attractive woman is commonly used to lots of attention and lots of effort on the part of her suitors. Human nature at work, Right? Of course. The point here is that "high maintenance" simply means she has inherently selfish tendencies because she can get away with being selfish. A woman who never takes the initiative to unlock your car door, or place value on your time and money, does so because she can and there is rarely a consequence to her actions. Remember how important empathy is as a character trait? The more selfish or 'internal' women lack the ability to see the world through your eyes. Don't jump to conclusions with this analogy, however. This unwanted behavior could be any woman, but generally speaking, attractive girls get more attention than average, so more pretty women tend to succumb to self-involved behavior. Avoid women who never take initiative and feel that it's "the man's job to make sure I'm happy". That's one of the biggest myths in the relationship world. Too many women are under the false belief that relationships really work this way. It makes for bad sex, too. Maybe it's from observing past behaviors like Mom and Dad, their peers, or your adolescent and teenage friends. Problem is, there are too many women still subscribing to it. This form of selfish behavior cuts both ways, however. If you see versions of this in your own behavior, all the more reason to learn how to rid yourself of this demon. Why put yourself through the stress of always being the performer, the leader, and the entertainment director of every relationship you enter. Resist the temptation to spoil her with full-time performances. You must allow her intellect to shine through. Remember, women have brains, imagination and talents just like you. It's OK to kick back every once in a while and let her take the wheel, so to speak.

With this new age of empowered women, keep in mind that there are some women that view men as "competition". This is a tough one to deal with because women often don't examine their own faulty behavior. Healthy competition is fine, but a good relationship has no competitors. We all have an ego that needs to be fed, but you must learn to identify what is healthy and what is destructive. Our friend Don, the dominant introvert, actually developed a test, so to speak, to weed out women who sabotage relationships by competing in the wrong arenas. What I mean here is that we all have strengths and weaknesses. Some of us have vast knowledge and skills in certain fields or endeavors, and you need to know what her strengths are, because the reigns of control need to be handed over to her sometimes. On the same note, she must know too. Don, as an avid outdoorsmen, had spent hundreds of hours on the river canoeing, and most of the women he took on these jaunts down the river were highly receptive. Don, knowing he was the experienced expert in this case, took control as he should, but he discovered that some women resisted and went into the compete mode, though they were the fish out of water. Arguments would ensue, with his dates challenging his decisions, his actions, his instructions. Kind of strange, but true. Don's only conclusion about these women was that they had a maturity deficiency and could not control their urge to compete, regardless of the situation. This "test" proved to be very effective in the future. According to Don, only about two out of ten (twenty percent) of the women he dated had "competition issues". Anyway, make sure you can recognize women that will compete at all costs and seem just a little too motivated to compete with you in this irrational way. This is a red flag. Recognize it and move on.

It is quite common too, that women often look at you, understand your weaknesses, visualize you without them, and take you on as their 'project'. The more the relationship progresses, the more potential she will see in you, and the more she will use her talents to control the outcome, which, in her mind, is a better you. Another red flag, my friend. I know sometimes walking away is hard, but you must understand that you are doomed when you fall into this type of relationship. Many great men throughout history achieved their status because of the woman (or women) in their lives, but there is a difference. These men were never a project. Their inspiration came from within as a result of a strong, supportive relationship. Your motivation to take yourself in a new direction always has to come from within. Look for a woman that inspires you, one that makes you want to go down new paths. The little voice that commands these changes for the better cannot be hers. It has to be yours. If you truly become a student of human nature, a woman's agenda should be apparent to you early on, and days, months, or years of misery can be avoided. As a dominant male, non-desirable behavior is easily spotted, and, instead of taking the hit on your confidence and self esteem, you will simply move on in the vast ocean of opportunity you've created. Here's the simplest of all truths:

A GOOD RELATIONSHIP INVOLVES TWO PEOPLE
WHO ARE HIGHLY MOTIVATED TO PLEASE,
OPENLY PROJECTING THEIR FEELINGS WITH AN
ALMOST BRUTAL HONESTY.

Sounds like common sense, but every five seconds

another man becomes a victim and enters into a doomed relationship(and vice versa). By motivated, I mean "willing". Willing to do what it takes(unselfish behavior) to understand and learn about your partner and what makes them tick. If you think you can buy a woman with jewelry and cars, think again. That's an agenda you don't have to deal with now. Once you've mastered the art of dominance and you know you have more choices, it becomes very empowering. Your self-esteem can't even be scratched, much less dented. In fact, you may find some women taking an immediate dislike to you as your behavior modifications take hold. Why? Well, it's simple. Many women play games and use manipulation to promote their own self-interests. They associate with men they feel they can use to their advantage. That means attempting to use you. Problem is, your understanding of human nature allows you to see through the layers of deceit. Your "street smarts" and new confidence easily expose her intimidating or controlling nature, and if she feels she can't control you, she simply won't associate with you. But don't fret, my friend. This type of female is bad news to begin with, no matter what appearances are. There is strength in numbers, so you can move on knowing you have the numbers on your side. It sounds a little heartless, but better some damage now than a world of hurt down the road.

I once heard a successful man say "I just treat everyone I meet the way I would want to be treated myself". Couldn't have said it better myself. If a woman has a strong desire to learn all there is to know about you and takes initiative to "feel" what you feel as you travel the road of life, chances are excellent you will be drawn towards her. So it stands to reason, if you do the same, she will be attracted to you and want to become closer to you.

CAVEATS/Warnings

Even More Pitfalls

the Dating Male Can Easily Fall Into

What your father told you to do," Go out and **get** yourself a girl."

We know that your Dad was well intentioned, however there is a world of misunderstanding imbedded in that statement. Men, tending to be overtly aggressive and thinking that they are expected to be aggressive tend to take a comment like that to heart. The thing is, you do not overtly, "get yourself a girl". You **present yourself** to your prospective girl. That's really all you can do. And really, once you get used to the idea, well it can be a great stress reducer if you keep things in proper perspective.

"When it's easy, it's easy!" I heard someone once say. The proper context of this statement is that when you present yourself to your prospective mate, things tend to go smoothly. In others words, being completely unpretentious (being yourself) and being comfortable with portraying the real you should always feel smooth and relaxed. If your female counterpart responds in an uncomfortable or pretentious manner, perhaps she's not worth the effort? In addition, to not take things lightly could easily lead you to fall victim to another pitfall.

The Myth of the One

Pair bonding is an extremely powerful drive. This is nature's way of getting us together to produce children. It also has other names, like 'falling in love', or 'infatuation'. Being in love has also been called other things; like 'a fine madness', or 'crazy in love'. Perhaps without denigrating the idea of love, you should consider the myth of the One. The romantic idea of The One, is where there is only one true love for any given person. Therefore, as the romantic myth goes, we are doomed to roam the earth looking for this mythological person. This concept has pursued us throughout the ages. Even in ancient Greek mythology, one of the Gods separated men and women to forever roam the Earth in search of each other. But this presumes that the original complete human being had two backs! And yet, if you were to go on a cruise or trip around the world, you will easily meet five women who are perfect for you. So, so much for the 'One' and shame on you if you obsess too much over one person. Especially if they do not readily return your attentions. As you grow into your dominant role, keep in mind that more discipline is required on your part. Specifically, the discipline to recognize your own obsessive (unbalanced) behavior and adjust the path you are on to a more emotionally healthy one.

The Satellite Syndrome

You meet a woman, she is somewhat attentive and definitely friendly. However, as things progress, (or seem to) you start to notice other men in her life. Not just her Dad and her brothers, but Joe and Jim and so forth. They are 'just friends' she may helpfully inform you. This may be so, however, you may have just entered into the her orbit as a satellite! The problem with being a satellite is that you will be required to devote yourself wholly to the 'Mother Planet' and it will be impossible for her to reciprocate **in kind**. And to make the assumption that she will want to is erroneous, no matter what she tells you. Ultimately she will accommodate you only enough to string you along. This type of person is ruled by their ego and an overindulgent need for attention and support. They will gather as many men into their orbit as possible. For you, true intimacy will not be possible, so say goodby to being the dominant male if you fall into this pursuit. Women who are highly self-involved are used to the performing males, and in their quest for attention, more is often better. To cater to this behavior is to drop down to the level of a performer, and your goal is to move up the scale, not down.

The Marilyn Monroe Syndrome

Closely linked to the Satellite Syndrome, this woman shares many traits. The need for attention is there, but in her quest for attention, she will ultimately sacrifice everything. The Marilyn girl is often outrageous in dress and appearance, with a predisposition towards exhibitionism. She may appear fun and intriguing, at first.

The Marilyn girl has charisma, give her that, but outside the sexual arena, she's trouble. Sex, to her, is control. She loves with all her heart, but because of her narcissistic traits and her inability to understand real love, she tends to use men. Remember what we said about balance, and understand that this girl leans heavily towards the unbalanced, obsessive compulsive side. As a result of her unbalanced nature, she will seek out balanced, 'anchored' men, latching on like a Titanic victim to a life raft. The Marilyn girl typifies self-indulgence and lack of character, and will often blame everyone but herself for her difficulties. Remember, as you improve your understanding of what attraction really is, this woman becomes easy to spot. Trouble is, all men, including you, have an immediate attraction to women that are outwardly sexual. That's not a bad thing, mind you. It becomes a problem only when sexual fantasy and expression override your ability to see past your immediate future with this girl. It's hard to come to grips with, I know, but you must walk away from her for the sake of your own sanity.

The Resistance Theory and the Non-Conformist

Everyone (men and women) needs challenges. However, they usually have an idea of the amount of resistance to their chosen challenge. For example, Do you think that the Princess of Monaco would be interested in your advances?

Or, is that crack-whore down in the business district looking good today? By considering these extremes you see how this works for you. But how does it work for her? If you are a Loner; against the established order, or otherwise highly individualistic, start toning it down. These traits can be very attractive to a woman, but a guy can go too far and they often do. Women realize that we live in a society and usually draw the line in going to war with the planet or moving to a deserted island. Being an anti-establishment James Dean works for you only if you appear to be genuinely friendly and comfortable around people in general. Being a loner in spirit is fine, but you still must inherit all five of the Carerra traits we covered earlier. Remember, a rich man can be called eccentric while a poor man is just crazy. What can you afford?

Finding "The Good Ones"

What defines a good woman? How do you recognize true inner beauty once the outside parameters are established and you have managed to peak her interest in you? Well, my friend, fret not, for the good ones are just as easy to spot. By now you should have some type of value system in place, but don't think the principles of behavior outlined in this book only apply to you. You should actively seek out women with the same understanding of you that you have. After all, there are plenty of women who understand men and their nature, and are willing to accept you for who you are, not for what you can potentially become. As you expand your intellect and begin understanding women's behavior, your preferences will probably change. You will look deeper, and, more than ever, start to appreciate women who are strong and wise beyond their years. Pretentious and selfish behavior will become easy to spot, and these truly beautiful gems will shine through like a beacon. The terms 'down to earth' and 'real' are used to describe these women, and they often have many of the same characteristics of dominant men. They are generally confident and comfortable with themselves. The next time you meet a woman, be aware of her characteristics, her body movements, her gestures, and her comfort level with you. All women (and men) have insecurities, but a girl that displays more natural behavior, even with modest looks, will attract men. After all, she, like you, is in balance, and has accepted, as you should, the issues of what can be controlled and what cannot. Opposites do often attract, but be careful of the criteria used here, because there is no formula that guarantees success. Selfish and self-centered people are always attracted to unselfish, thoughtful people. This by no means suggests a good foundation for a relationship. In short, I will tell you to look for a woman who matches your passions in life, can identify and understand your dreams, and promotes the concept of you being yourself in her presence. When this happens to you, and you find this woman, you will know, and your search will be over.

Your 'To Do' List

Many new ideas, concepts, and principles have been introduced to you throughout your journey to the core of human behavior. I know that inside you there is an interest in what you are discovering by reading this book. Interest is good, but it must eventually be translated into some form of action. It's gut check time now, and you have to decide whether or not you want to be a spectator or a player in the game of life. Your new knowledge and understanding of male/female behavior must be applied. The worst thing any man can do, and that means you, my friend, is not even try to reach your god-given potential. You have talents. Decide now that you want to control the fear of change and leave your old persona behind.

There is absolutely no way to guide you when it comes to the use of your imagination. Jerry Lewis never took a class or read a book on 'How to be Funny". Creativity comes from within you. It has your personal stamp. There are, however, tangible steps you can take, every day, to gain forward momentum. All the traits and behaviors you are aware of now must be applied. Think of it as a 'to do' list for your personal growth.

1. Feed your own confidence by staying in control.

2. Stop letting fear control you.

3. Strengthen the weaknesses in your character.

4. Be more sociable, more approachable, and friendly.

5. Be pro-active in your behavior.

6. Find your passion and allow it to intensify.

7. Enjoy the journey that is your life.

8. Learn to compliment women.

9. Become a better listener.

10. Develop friendships with more women.

11. Expose your weaknesses and your passions to more women.

12. Resist the urge to perform. Be yourself.

13. Leave your comfort zone intentionally.

14. Approach women as though you will never have a second chance.

15. Learn to live and enjoy the moment.

16. Trust your instincts.

17. Be your own man. Stop being a slave to the rest of the world.

18. Stop caring about other peoples' evaluations of you.

19. Stop making excuses for what you know to be poor habits.

20. Think before you talk.

21. Bring balance into your life.

Finally

What are most single men in America doing at this moment in time? Do you think they are consciously trying to improve on weaknesses they know they have? Of course not. If it ain't broke why fix it? Right? I tell you this because you are a rare individual. Even as you read, you inch your way up the scale. You have forward momentum. Keep it moving. I guarantee that your conscious efforts will be rewarded. Let us review the traits that will be part of your essence from this point forward.

How confident are you? How do you carry yourself at this moment in time? Jack Palance, the actor, once said "Confidence is very sexy....don't you think?" That quote was dead on. It's time you leave your comfort zone. Think about a time in your life when your confidence was at its pinnacle. Take the steps you need to take to get there again.

Can you put your ego aside and really listen and absorb what a woman tells you? Empathy is essential. Why are so many women drawn to gay men? It's not the lack of sexual tension. It's identification. They can relate Being able to listen and identify with someone is what will gain you many new female friends. You need to learn a new language, so to speak.

How often do you smile? How often do you laugh? How approachable are you? Notice, the next time you have a visual on several attractive women, that the one who is laughing and smiling is the one that draws your attention. How odd? So, what will you do with the situation reversed? That's right. Let the other men be stone-faced and cool. You are there to enjoy and to be enjoyed. So smile, laugh, and shake off some of those male stereotype behaviors.

Are you a good loser? Do you laugh at yourself when you are the only witness to a personal mishap? Humility is quite rare, indeed. But the ladies love this trait in a man. It's that sonar at work again. Like a tell in poker, you give away the essence of your character, your class, and your role as a lover, a father, and a companion to her. And, believe me, it's all good.

Passion, on its own, is sexy. Think about it. When a romantic leading man exclaims to a woman, "I miss you. I can't wait to kiss you again", has the woman ever been repulsed? Of course not. Would the average Joe get the same results. Of course he will. Anyone who advertises desire is sexy. When you hunger for more, like a child's outward curiosity of everything and anything, you are the benefactor. Understand?

Confidence, empathy, friendliness, humility, and passion are the essential ingredients you will need moving forward. It is important that you do not emulate others with these traits. Develop your own style, use your own imagination and creativeness, and soon you will feel like it was nature's intention for you to be the dominant man you have become.

In closing, let's remember that there is absolutely no one method, form of behavior, or subtle smalltalk that is guaranteed, and what may work with one woman certainly will not be effective on another. What worked in 1960 won't fly today. Women are more empowered and independent than ever before, and this is a blessing if you can achieve dominant qualities in your behavior. Why? Well, let's look at the issue of control. Less has become more. Independent, free thinking women resist total control by anyone. But that's a good thing. Now you can just relax and be yourself. There are still a lot of "southern belles" out there, but now, with your rise in dominance, the power of choice is in your hands. So get to it, my rising star. Remember, your goal is to expand in small increments, slowly and steadily, until you are satisfied with your new sex appeal. Learn as much as you can about human behavior, for that will dictate changes in your behavior. There are publications that deal specifically with the art of seduction, dressing for success, and even body language and how to read it. Don't stop here. Your mind is an organ you can exercise, and with exercise, you stay ahead of the competition, but more importantly, you start to identify all human behavior, and, believe me, there is great personal comfort in understanding every person who walks, talks, and gestures in your presence. The next time you are out socially think about what you've just absorbed, how empowering it feels, and how confident you feel knowing even a little more about behavior and identifying what you could never see before.

You, as well as every other human being with normal intelligence, have great potential. Everything you want to accomplish demands your mental discipline be tested and pushed beyond the level where it now exists. Like an old saying explains, 'I have led you to the water, now you must take the drink'. Think of everything you have read up to this point. From the standpoint of pure logic, it should make sense to you. You study and learn, then begin to apply, and the end result is improvement in you and your love life. Done deal. But you can't cut corners. You can have dozen's of women fantasizing about being with you, with an appeal factor of a Hollywood leading man , but if you can't hold on to what is drawn to you, you lose. It's time to open that blind eye and truly examine your own shortcomings. Admit you have faults, identify what they are, and work on yourself as an ongoing project. A project that will never be completed. So go forth and enjoy the journey – revel in it, have fun with it, and learn from it. Good luck and good fortune will most certainly find you.

ABOUT THE AUTHORS

Jim Carrera and Sean Marsh began a small study of human attraction in 1978 as two college graduates with an interest in men who were highly successful with women. Though only in their twenties at the time, they began to determine why some men struggle with their effort to attract women and others seem to attract women effortlessly. Sean Marsh, after earning his masters, teamed up with Jim Carrera again in 1980 to study a small test group of men for common traits that make them successful with women. The effort was considered to be successful for a standardized Psychological study, but the only determining factors were the social, cultural, and personality classifications of these men. In 1981, Jim and Sean teamed up again for a long term study of male dominance, this time using a more unconventional approach. Their goal was to observe the involuntary, primitive human behavior without cultural or social influences. This was a break-through study in the field of Psychology, and the first of its kind to analyze human instincts in relation to sexual attraction and male dominance. The discovery that physical appearance and personality play only secondary roles explains why so many publications meant to help men have failed. In 2001, with a twenty year study of male dominance completed, Jim and Sean collaborated again for the publication of the common behaviors of dominant men along with a roadmap to achieve male dominance and success with women. The result is 'The Tao of Male Sex Appeal'.

Printed in the United States
142232LV00001B/37/A